RILKE
on Love and Other
Difficulties

RILKE

on Love and Other Difficulties

Translations and Considerations of
RAINER MARIA RILKE

—

John J. L. Mood

W · W · NORTON & COMPANY · INC ·

NEW YORK

FIRST EDITION

✳ This book was typeset in Linotype Caledonia by Spartan Typographers. Offset printing was done by the Murray Printing Company.

Library of Congress Cataloging in Publication Data
Rilke, Rainer Maria, 1875–1926.
    Rilke on love and other difficulties.
    Selections from letters and essays in English;
poems in English and German.
    I. Mood, John L., ed.   II. Title.
PT2635.I65A6 1975   831'.9'12   74–6012
ISBN 0–393–04390–8

1 2 3 4 5 6 7 8 9 0

to
S.R.H.
&
F.W.P.

for
S.L.E.

CONTENTS

—

Contents

Contents

ACKNOWLEDGMENTS

———

THE PROSE SELECTIONS included here are taken from *Letters to a Young Poet*, rev. ed., trans. by M. D. Herter Norton (New York: W. W. Norton, 1954), *Letters of Rainer Maria Rilke*, 2 vols., trans. by Jane Bannard Greene and M. D. Herter Norton (New York: W. W. Norton, 1945, 1948), *The Notebooks of Malte Laurids Brigge*, trans. by M. D. Herter Norton (New York: W. W. Norton, 1949), *Selected Works*, vol. I, *Prose*, trans. by G. Craig Houston (London: Hogarth, 1954), *Letters to Benvenuta*, trans. by Heinz Norden (London: Hogarth, 1953), and *Letters to Merline*, trans. by Violet M. MacDonald (London: Methuen, 1951).

All poetic selections included here are my translations from the definitive collection, *Sämtliche Werke* (Insel-Verlag), vol. I (1955), vol. II (1956). In the German text, one will find occasional brackets. These indicate words or lines later canceled by Rilke.

Some of my translations, as well as earlier versions and portions thereof, have appeared in the following journals: *New York Quarterly, Philosophy Today, Encounter, Bucks County Gazette,* and *South.*

If only we arrange our life according
to that principle which counsels us
that we must always hold to the difficult,
then that which now still seems to us
the most alien will become what we
most trust and find most faithful.

I. Prologue

IT IS MY CONVICTION THAT, by any measure, the two greatest writers of the twentieth century are James Joyce
(1882–1941) and Rainer Maria Rilke (1875–1926),
neither of whom came close to winning the Nobel Prize for
Literature. I mention that last fact because I too find it
difficult to say anything appropriate about either of them,
though no doubt for different reasons than those of the
Nobel Committee. Frequently it takes time to appreciate
more fully and appropriately a great writer's work. In fact,
the closer I am to a writer's work and the more I love it,
just so the more difficult is it for me to speak of it. Because
of Rilke's importance to my own biography, I find it most
difficult of all to speak of him. But as there is a time to be
silent, so there is a time to speak. And I have become increasingly compelled to speak Rilke's work. After a decade
and a half of living with it, speaking that work has become
an inner necessity for me.

This conflict between the difficulty of speaking and the
necessity for doing so only slowly produced words. The
first result for me was a selection dealing with love from
Rilke's letters. I arranged these selections into what seemed
to me some order under the lackadaisical title "Notes on
Love," mimeographed it and gave copies to friends, stu-
dents, loved ones, and others. I have no idea how many
copies of it I handed out over the period of nearly a decade. But those were Rilke's words, not mine, though my own
sense of Rilke and my own sensibility in general surely
manifested themselves in the selection and arrangement of
the essay.

The second result was occasional reference to Rilke and
translation of lines of his poetry in articles of mine on other
topics. It was as though I could only speak his work indi-

rectly, in other contexts. This too continued over the years.

Then, some time back, I suddenly found myself feverishly translating some of the last poems of Rilke. I spent nearly a month at that task, which overrode all my other responsibilities at the time. Halfway through that seizure I realized what had precipitated it: I had just finished teaching, for the second or third time, Rilke's profound and beautiful novel, *The Notebooks of Malte Laurids Brigge*. But the seizure soon passed, I put the poems away, and there was another pause, another silence.

Finally, while recently rereading some of Rilke again (an almost constant activity of mine), the necessity became overpowering and I had to speak. This book is the result. It includes all the previously mentioned material, somewhat revised, plus further translations and short essays. I am not satisfied with it. My translations are, of course, inadequate. My own words seem partial. I have not found it possible to speak the deeper dimensions of my sense of Rilke, which is somehow very close to my ownmost biography and being. Here are only fragments, portions—emphasizing elements from my own experience of Rilke which seem to have been neglected by others or which are less private favorite moments of mine.

However inadequate, these words are offered in love to other Rilke-lovers, who no doubt have their own more private and secret moments, as do I—moments of awesome mystery, impossible to speak. It is for the possibility of further such moments, full of serenity and dread, that this book is presented.

II. Letters on Love

INTRODUCTION

I FIRST MADE the following selection almost ten years ago. Around 1960 I discovered Simone de Beauvoir's *The Second Sex* and immediately became a militant feminist, as we were called in those days. At the same time, I had been reading Rilke casually for several years. That reading became more serious and comprehensive, and as it did I became increasingly aware that Rilke had not only anticipated Mlle. de Beauvoir by fifty years but had also gone far, far beyond her, and all the other women's liberation advocates, as they are now called, as well. As good as her monumental study was, it stayed finally at the level of a socio-politico-physiological analysis of Western woman. And it was finally a masculine book with the masculine goal of freedom and equality as its primary focus. Which is not to gainsay either its contemporary relevance or final importance. But I have an incurably metaphysical mind, and I was not finally satisfied with her book. It unwittingly raised more questions than it answered, and the questions raised seemed somehow the deeper ones: questions of the ontology of the sexes, of what finally and at the deepest level the feminine is, of what being-human is, of what, most importantly, love is.

On the other hand, Rilke, as I discovered more and more, immediately went to these deepest levels, especially of the mythic nature of the feminine and of love, while not relinquishing the insights of the feminists themselves (among whom one of the earliest important figures, Ellen Key, was his friend, and among whom one of the greatest and most fantastic and, be it said, most neurotic, exemplars, Lou Andreas-Salomé, was his lover as well as lifelong friend). His working toward love at these depths was poetic, profound, and above all thoroughly radical. One of the amazing things about Rilke is that he started at the place where most of us at best manage finally to end up. An example of the radical nature of his inquiry is his almost by-the-way rejection of all conventionality of any kind, whether moral or "in the ordinary sense immoral." As he softly but strikingly said, "In the depths all becomes law." Other examples are his casual comments on happiness, his sense of the current absence of the gods and their eventual return, and his understanding of solitude and the provisional nature of being human.

This process of exploring love and what was happening with it in our time, and especially as manifested in the feminine, resulted in some surprising things regarding the masculine as well, to say nothing of the relation between art and sex or of the sexual experience of the young. And all of this was done through the most beautiful and provocative metaphors, primarily those of growth and of sex. It should be emphasized that Rilke's language is thoroughly sensual throughout all his writings. There is probably no more sensual poet in any language. All of his metaphors, his "figures," have deliberate sexual undertones (or overtones). The same holds true for his letters. Rilke's justly famed deep spirituality is rooted finally and forever in the earth, in the senses, in sex. In fact, a close reading will manifest a surprising relationship toward sex between Rilke and Norman Mailer, whose approach, especially in *The Prisoner of Sex,* is ostensibly so different.

To share my regard for this dimension of Rilke, I prepared, as I have said, the following selection from his voluminous letters. Letter writing was Rilke's mode of exploration during the long periods between his well-known great creative bursts of poetry. And because he was not a systematic thinker (but was a profound one for all that), his writings on love and the feminine were scattered. I have brought them together here and arranged them in what is, I think, a unified essay—suggestive and subtle, but with a definite progression nonetheless. I am convinced that these words of Rilke are of crucial importance for us who have, in the words of someone (I forget who), passed from puritanism to promiscuity without ever having experienced genuine love, *erōs*, deep sensuality, what Suzanne Lilar (an unjustly ignored feminine thinker) called sacral love.

This is not a complete selection of Rilke's writings on the topic by any means, but other passages could not be easily fitted into the unified essay. One such passage might be quoted here because of its importance and by way of introduction to the essay:

So I began to read [an essay on love], yesterday, but did not get very far. What is this curious mixture of virtuosity and incapacity they call by that name here (and cannot mention often enough)? On the one hand the most exquisite skill, on the other everlasting frustration. Do you know what I felt like, leafing through Plato's *Symposium* for the first time in a long while? When I first read it, I dwelt alone in Rome in a tiny house deep in an ancient park (the same house where I began *Brigge*, as yet unaware of what was to become of it). My friend, I grasped one thing then, predisposed as I may have been—there is no beauty in Eros; and when Socrates said so and in his cautious way waited for his younger and more volatile conversational antagonist to block all other paths, one by one, leaving but the one way open—that Eros is not beautiful —Socrates himself then walking that path toward his god, serene and pure in heart—how then my innermost nature took fire that Eros could not be fair! I saw him just as Socrates had invoked him, lean and hard and always a little out of breath, sleepless, troubled day and night about the two between whom he trod, to and fro, hither and yon, ceaselessly accosted by both: yes, that was Eros. Truly, how they mistook him who thought he was fair, envied his soft life. Ah, he was slender and tanned and covered with the dust of the road, but there was no peace for him amid the two of them (for when, I say, is there not distance left between them?); and when he came he spoke with fervor of the other's beauty, teasing each heart to grow fairer, goading it on. Surely there is much in the book—we do not grasp it yet: once upon a time it *was* grasped—who lost it? How do we spend the centuries? Where is he among us who dare speak of *love?*

Verily, nature speaks not of love; nature bears it in her heart and none knows the heart of nature. Verily, God bears love in the world, yet the world overwhelms us. Verily, the mother speaks not of love, for it is borne for her within the child, and the child destroys it. Verily, the spirit speaks not of love, for the spirit thrusts it into the future, and the future is remote. Verily, the lover speaks not of love, for to the lover it comes in sorrow, and sorrow sheds tears.

Who has yet answered these questions? Who has *thought,* seriously, that there is no beauty in Eros? And especially, who dares speak at all of love? Rilke did—and if he found no final answers, he unquestionably gestured toward some hitherto unexplored but increasingly fruitful paths.

A final word: most of the following was written when Rilke was only in his late twenties; and, even more surprising, the first sentence of it was written when Rilke was forty-five.

RILKE'S LETTERS ON LOVE

I tell you that I have a long way to go before I am—where one begins. . . .

You are so young, so before all beginning, and I want to beg you, as much as I can, to be patient toward all that is unsolved in your heart and to try to love the *questions themselves* like locked rooms and like books that are written in a very foreign tongue. Do not now seek the answers, which cannot be given you because you would not be able to live them. And the point is, to live everything. *Live* the questions now. Perhaps you will then gradually, without noticing it, live along some distant day into the answer.

Resolve to be always beginning—to be a beginner!

Here, in the love which, with an intolerable mixture of contempt, desire, and curiosity, they call "sensual," here indeed are to be found the worst results of that vilification of earthly life which Christianity has felt obliged to engage in. Here everything is distorted and disowned, although it is from this deepest of all events that we come forth, and have ourselves the centre of our ecstasies in it. It seems to me, if I may say so, more and more incomprehensible that a doctrine which puts us in the wrong in *that* matter, where the whole creation enjoys its most blissful right, should be able, if not anywhere to prove its validity, at least to assert itself over a wide area.

Why, I ask you, when people want to help us, who are so often helpless, why do they leave us in the lurch just there, at the root of all experience? Anyone who would stand by us *there* could rest satisfied that we should ask nothing further from him. For the help which he imparted to us there would grow of itself with our life, becoming, together with it, greater and stronger. And would never fail. Why are we not set in the midst of what is most mysteriously ours? How we have to creep round about it and get into it in the end; like burglars and thieves, we get into our own beautiful sex, in which we lose our way and knock ourselves and stumble and finally rush out of it again, like men caught transgressing, into the twilight of Christianity. Why, if guilt or sin had to be invented because of the inner tension of the spirit, why did they not attach it to some other part of our body, why did they let it fall on that part, waiting till it dissolved in our pure source and poisoned and muddied it? Why have they made our sex homeless, instead of making it the place for the festival of our competency?

Very well, I will allow that it should not belong to us, who are not able to answer for and administer such inexhaustible bliss. But why do we not belong to God from *this* point?

A churchman would point out to me that there is marriage, although he is not unaware of the state of affairs in respect of that institution. It does not help either to put the will to propagation within the sphere of grace—my sex is not directed only toward posterity, it is the secret of my own life—and it is only, it seems, because it may not occupy the central place there, that so many people have thrust it to the edge, and thereby lost their balance. What good is it all? The terrible untruthfulness and uncertainty of our age has its roots in the refusal to acknowledge the happiness of sex, in this peculiarly mistaken guilt, which constantly increases, separating us from the rest of nature, even from the child, although his, the child's, innocence does not consist at all in the fact that he does not know sex, so to say—but that incomprehensible happiness, which awakens for us at *one* place deep within the pulp of a close embrace, is still present anonymously in every part of his body. In order to describe the peculiar situation of our sensual appetite we should have to say: Once we were children in every part, now we are that in one part only. But if there were only one among us for whom this was a certainty and who was capable of providing proof of it, why do we allow it to happen that generation after generation awakens to consciousness beneath the rubble of Christian prejudices and moves like the seemingly dead in the darkness, in a most narrow space between sheer abnegations!?

I hold this to be the highest task of a bond between two people: that each should stand guard over the solitude of the other. For, if it lies in the nature of indifference and of the crowd to recognize no solitude, then love and friendship are there for the purpose of continually providing the opportunity for solitude. And only those are the true sharings which rhythmically interrupt periods of deep isolation. . . .

I am of the opinion that "marriage" as such does not deserve as much emphasis as it has acquired through the conventional development of its nature. It does not occur to anyone to expect a single person to be "happy,"—but if he marries, people are much surprised if he *isn't!* (And for that matter it really isn't at all important to be happy, whether single or married.) Marriage is, in many respects, a simplification of one's way of life, and the union naturally combines the forces and wills of two young people so that, together, they seem to reach farther into the future than before.—Only, those are sensations by which one cannot live. Above all, marriage is a new task and a new seriousness,—a new challenge to and questioning of the strength

27

and generosity of each partner and a great new danger for both.

It is a question in marriage, to my feeling, not of creating a quick community of spirit by tearing down and destroying all boundaries, but rather a good marriage is that in which each appoints the other guardian of his solitude, and shows him this confidence, the greatest in his power to bestow. A *togetherness* between two people is an impossibility, and where it seems, nevertheless, to exist, it is a narrowing, a reciprocal agreement which robs either one party or both of his fullest freedom and development. But, once the realization is accepted that even between the *closest* human beings infinite distances continue to exist, a wonderful living side by side can grow up, if they succeed in loving the distance between them which makes it possible for each to see the other whole and against a wide sky!

Therefore this too must be the standard for rejection or choice: whether one is willing to stand guard over the solitude of a person and whether one is inclined to set this same person at the gate of one's own solitude, of which he learns only through that which steps, festively clothed, out of the great darkness.

At bottom no one in life can help anyone else in life; this one experiences over and over in every conflict and every perplexity: that one is alone.

All companionship can consist only in the strengthening of two neighboring solitudes, whereas everything that one is wont to call giving oneself is by nature harmful to companionship: for when a person abandons himself, he is no longer anything, and when two people both give themselves up in order to come close to each other, there is no longer any ground beneath them and their being together is a continual falling.

There is scarcely anything more difficult than to love one another. That it is work, day labor, day labor, God knows there is no other word for it. And look, added to this is the fact that young people are not prepared for such difficult loving; for convention has tried to make this most complicated and ultimate relationship into something easy and frivolous, has given it the appearance of everyone's being able to do it. It is not so. Love is something difficult and it is more difficult than other things because in other conflicts nature herself enjoins men to collect themselves, to take themselves firmly in hand with all their strength, while in the heightening of love the impulse is to give oneself wholly away. But just think, can that be anything beautiful, to give oneself away not as something whole and ordered, but haphazard rather, bit by bit, as it comes? Can such giving away, that looks so like a throwing away and dismemberment, be anything good, can it be happiness, joy, progress? No, it cannot. . . . When you give someone flowers, you arrange them beforehand, don't you? But young people who love each other fling themselves to each other in the impatience and haste of their passion, and they don't notice at all what a lack of mutual esteem lies in this disordered giving of themselves; they notice it with astonishment and indignation only from the dissension that arises between them out of all this disorder. And once there is disunity between them, the confusion grows with every day; neither of the two has anything unbroken, pure, and unspoiled about him any longer, and amid the disconsolateness of a break they try to hold fast to the semblance of their happiness (for all that was really supposed to be for the sake of happiness). Alas, they are scarcely able to recall any more what they meant by happiness. In his uncertainty each becomes more and more unjust toward the other; they who wanted to do each other good are now handling one another in an imperious and intolerant manner, and in the struggle somehow to get out of their untenable and unbearable state of confusion, they commit the greatest fault that can happen to human relationships: they become impatient.

They hurry to a conclusion; to come, as they believe, to a final decision, they try once and for all to establish their relationship, whose surprising changes have frightened them, in order to remain the same now and *forever* (as they say). That is only the last error in this long chain of errings linked fast to one another. What is dead cannot even be clung to (for it crumbles and changes its character); how much less can what is living and alive be treated definitively, once and for all. Self-transformation is precisely what life is, and human relationships, which are an extract of life, are the most changeable of all, rising and falling from minute to minute, and lovers are those in whose relationship and contact no one moment resembles another. People between whom nothing accustomed, nothing that has already been present before ever takes place, but many new, unexpected, unprecedented things. There are such relationships which must be a very great, almost unbearable happiness, but they can occur only between very rich natures and between those who, each for himself, are richly ordered and composed; they can unite only two wide, deep, individual worlds.—Young people—it is obvious—cannot achieve such a relationship, but they can, if they understand their life properly, grow up slowly to such happiness and prepare themselves for it. They must not forget, when they love, that they are beginners, bunglers of life, apprentices in love,—must *learn* love, and that (like *all* learning) wants peace, patience, and composure!

To take love seriously and to bear and to learn it like a task, this it is that young people need.—Like so much else, people have also misunderstood the place of love in life, they have made it into play and pleasure because they thought that play and pleasure were more blissful than work; but there is nothing happier than work, and love, just because it is the extreme happiness, can be nothing else but work.—So whoever loves must try to act as if he had a great work: he must be much alone and go into himself and collect himself and hold fast to himself; he must work; he must become something!

For believe me, the more one is, the richer is all that one experiences. And whoever wants to have a deep love in his life must collect and save for it and gather honey.

To love is good, too: love being difficult. For one human being to love another: that is perhaps the most difficult of all our tasks, the ultimate, the last test and proof, the work for which all other work is but preparation. For this reason young people, who are beginners in everything, cannot yet know love: they have to learn it. With their whole being, with all their forces, gathered close about their lonely, timid, upward-beating heart, they must learn to love. But learning-time is always a long, secluded time, and so loving, for a long while ahead and far on into life, is—solitude, intensified and deepened loneness for him who loves. Love is at first not anything that means merging, giving over, and uniting with another (for what would a union be of something unclarified and unfinished, still subordinate—?); it is a high inducement to the individual to ripen, to become something in himself, to become world, to become world for himself for another's sake; it is a great exacting claim upon him, something that chooses him out and calls him to vast things. Only in this sense, as the task of working at themselves ("to hearken and to hammer day and night"), might young people use the love that is given them. Merging and surrendering and every kind of communion is not for them (who must save and gather for a long, long time still), is the ultimate, is perhaps that for which human lives as yet scarcely suffice.

But young people err so often and so grievously in this: that they (in whose nature it lies to have no patience) fling themselves at each other, when love takes possession of them, scatter themselves, just as they are, in all their untidiness, disorder, confusion. . . . And then what? What is life to do to this heap of half-battered existence which they call their communion and which they would gladly call their happiness, if it were possible, and their future? Thus each loses himself for the sake of the other and loses the other and many others that wanted still to come. And loses the expanses and the possibilities, exchanges the approach and flight of gentle, divining things for an unfruitful perplexity out of which nothing can come any more, nothing save a little disgust, disillusionment and poverty, and rescue in one of the many conventions that have been put up in great number like public refuges along this most dangerous road. No realm of human experience is so well provided with conventions as this: life-preservers of most varied invention, boats and swimming-bladders are here; the social conception has managed to supply shelters of every sort, for, as it was disposed to take love-life as a pleasure, it had also to give it an easy form, cheap, safe and sure, as public pleasures are.

It is true that many young people who wrongly, that is, simply with abandon and unsolitarily (the average will of course always go on doing so), feel the oppressiveness of a failure and want to make the situation in which they have landed viable and fruitful in their own personal way—; for their nature tells them that, less even than all else that is important, can questions of love be solved publicly and according to this or that agreement; that they are questions, intimate questions from one human being to another, which in any case demand a new, special, *only* personal answer—: but how should they, who have already flung themselves together and no longer mark off and distinguish themselves from each other, who therefore no longer possess anything of their own selves, be able to find a way out of themselves, out of the depth of their already shattered solitude?

They act out of common helplessness, and then, if, with the best intentions, they try to avoid the convention that occurs to them (say, marriage), they land in the tentacles of some less loud, but equally deadly conventional solution; for then everything far around them is—convention; where people act out of a prematurely fused, turbid communion, *every* move is convention: every relation to which such entanglement leads has its convention, be it ever so unusual (that is, in the ordinary sense immoral); why, even separation would here be a conventional step, an impersonal chance decision without strength and without fault.

Whoever looks seriously at it finds that neither for death, which is difficult, nor for difficult love has any explanation, any solution, any hint or way yet been discerned; and for these two problems that we carry wrapped up and hand on without opening, it will not be possible to discover any general rule resting in agreement. But in the same measure in which we begin as individuals to put life to the test, we shall, being individuals, meet these great things at closer range. The demands which the difficult work of love makes upon our development are more than life-size, and as beginners we are not up to them. But if we nevertheless hold out and take this love upon us as burden and apprenticeship, instead of losing ourselves in all the light and frivolous play, behind which people have hidden from the most earnest earnestness of their existence—then a little progress and an alleviation will perhaps be perceptible to those who come long after us; that would be much.

Sex is difficult; yes. But they are difficult things with which we have been charged; almost everything serious is difficult, and everything is serious. If you only recognize this and manage, out of yourself, out of your *own* nature and ways, out of your *own* experience and childhood and strength to achieve a relation to sex wholly your own (*not* influenced by convention and custom), then you need no longer be afraid of losing yourself and becoming unworthy of your best possession.

Physical pleasure is a sensual experience no different

from pure seeing or the pure sensation with which a fine fruit fills the tongue; it is a great unending experience, which is given us, a knowing of the world, the fullness and the glory of all knowing. And not our acceptance of it is bad; the bad thing is that most people misuse and squander this experience and apply it as a stimulant at the tired spots of their lives and as distraction instead of a rallying toward exalted moments. Men have made even eating into something else: want on the one hand, superfluity upon the other, have dimmed the distinctness of this need, and all the deep, simple necessities in which life renews itself have become similarly dulled. But the individual can clarify them for himself and live them clearly (and if not the individual, who is too dependent, then at least the solitary man). He can remember that all beauty in animals and plants is a quiet enduring form of love and longing, and he can see animals, as he sees plants, patiently and willingly uniting and increasing and growing, not out of physical delight, not out of physical suffering, but bowing to necessities that are greater than pleasure and pain and more powerful than will and withstanding. O that man might take this secret, of which the world is full even to its littlest things, more humbly to himself and bear it, endure it, more seriously and feel how terribly difficult it is, instead of taking it lightly. That he might be more reverent toward his fruitfulness, which is but *one,* whether it seems mental or physical; for intellectual creation too springs from the physical, is of one nature with it and only like a gentler, more ecstatic and more everlasting repetition of physical delight. "The thought of being creator, of procreating, of making" is nothing without its continuous great confirmation and realization in the world, nothing without the thousandfold concordance from things and animals—and enjoyment of it is so indescribably beautiful and rich only because it is full of inherited memories of the begetting and the bearing of millions. In one creative thought a thousand forgotten nights of love revive, filling

it with sublimity and exaltation. And those who come together in the night and are entwined in rocking delight do
an earnest work and gather sweetnesses, gather depth and
strength for the song of some coming poet, who will arise
to speak of ecstasies beyond telling. And they call up the
future; and though they err and embrace blindly, the future comes all the same, a new human being rises up, and
on the ground of that chance which here seems consum-
mated, awakes the law by which a resistant vigorous seed
forces its way through to the egg-cell that moves open
toward it. Do not be bewildered by the surfaces; in the
depths all becomes law. And those who live the secret wrong
and badly (and they are very many), lose it only for themselves and still hand it on, like a sealed letter, without
knowing it. And do not be confused by the multiplicity of
names and the complexity of cases. Perhaps over all there
is a great motherhood, as common longing. The beauty of
the virgin, a being that "has not yet achieved anything," is
motherhood that begins to sense itself and to prepare, anx-
ious and yearning. And the mother's beauty is ministering
motherhood, and in the old woman there is a great remembering. And even in the man there is motherhood, it seems
to me, physical and spiritual; his procreating is also a kind
of giving birth, and giving birth it is when he creates out
of inmost fullness. And pehaps the sexes are more related
than we think, and the great renewal of the world will perhaps consist in this, that man and maid, freed of all false
feelings and reluctances, will seek each other not as oppo-
sites but as brother and sister, as neighbors, and will come
together *as human beings,* in order simply, seriously and
patiently to bear in common the difficult sex that has been
laid upon them.

We are only just now beginning to look upon the relation of one individual person to a second individual objec-
tively and without prejudice, and our attempts to live such

associations have no model before them. And yet in the changes brought about by time there is already a good deal that would help our timorous novitiate.

You characterize very well with the term: "living and writing in heat."—*And* in fact artistic experience lies so incredibly close to that of sex, to its pain and its ecstasy, that the two manifestations are indeed but different forms of one and the same yearning and delight. And if instead of heat one might say—sex, sex in the great, broad, clean sense, free of any insinuation of ecclesiastical error, then art would be very grand and infinitely important. Poetic power is great, strong as a primitive instinct; it has its own unyielding rhythms in itself and breaks out as out of mountains.

But it seems that this power is not always honest and without pose. Where, as it rushes through his being, it comes to the sexual, it finds not quite so pure a man as it might require. Here is no thoroughly mature and clean sex world, but one that is not sufficiently *human,* that is only *male,* is heat, intoxication and restlessness, and laden with the old prejudices and arrogances with which man has disfigured and burdened love. Because he loves as man *only,* not as human being, for this reason there is in his sexual feeling something narrow, seeming wild, spiteful, time-bound, uneternal.

The girl and the woman, in their new, their own unfolding, will but in passing be imitators of masculine ways, good and bad, and repeaters of masculine professions. After the uncertainty of such transitions it will become apparent that women were only going through the profusion and the vicissitude of those (often ridiculous) disguises in order to cleanse their own most characteristic nature of the distorting influences of the other sex. Women, in whom life lingers and dwells more immediately, more fruitfully and more confidently, must surely have become fundamentally riper people, more human people, than easygoing man, who is not pulled down below the surface of life by the weight of any fruit of his body, and who, presumptuous and hasty, undervalues what he thinks he loves. This humanity of woman, borne its full time in suffering and humiliation, will come to light when she will have stripped off the conventions of mere femininity in the mutations of her outward status, and those men who do not yet feel it approaching today will be surprised and struck by it. Some day (and for this, particularly in the northern countries, reliable signs are already speaking and shining), some day there will be girls and women whose name will no longer signify merely an opposite of the masculine, but something in itself, something that makes one think, not of any complement and limit, but only of life and existence: the feminine human being.

This advance will (at first much against the will of the outstripped men) change the love-experience, which is now full of error, will alter it from the ground up, reshape it into a relation that is meant to be of one human being to another, no longer of man to woman. And this more human love (that will fulfill itself, infinitely considerate and gentle, and kind and clear in binding and releasing) will resemble that which we are preparing with struggle and toil, the love that consists in this, that two solitudes protect and border and salute each other.

We are anyway—do not forget it—entirely in the province of guiltlessness.—The terrifying thing is that we possess no religion in which these experiences, being so literal and palpable as they are (for: at the same time so inexpressible and so intangible), may be lifted up into the god, into the protection of a phallic deity who will perhaps have to be the *first* with which a troop of gods will again invade humanity, after so long an absence.

III. *Poems on Love*

INTRODUCTION

I HAVE SAID that there is perhaps no great poet whose work is more sensual than that of Rilke, that the great spirituality of his work is forever and always rooted in the senses. I think this is obvious in all of his poetry. The subject matter, the images, the undertones, the figures—all are earthly, even earthy in resonance. His concern with things is itself an illustration of this. And his fascination with and portrayal of the great lovers, especially women, is well known, as, for example, in *The Notebooks of Malte Laurids Brigge*. Even the *Duino Elegies,* in relation to which one thinks of many things—the angel, lamentation, praise, etc.—, includes a surprisingly large amount of sexual poetry. And Rilke's constant concern with death is another example, for what is more sensual and earthly than death? And we have seen some of this deep sensuality in his letters on love.

In spite of all this, however, few discussions of Rilke make anything at all of this specifically sexual dimension of his work. The reason, I think, is that his profound spirituality is so striking that commentators do not notice the sensual rootedness of that spirituality. The poems I have included here should redress the balance, for they are not only sensual but explicitly, even at times baldly, sexual. And yet all of Rilke's perennial themes are present in these poems. Notice, for example, that the "seven phallic poems" present practically every major Rilkean figure: rose, tree, night, tower, death, column, child, space, call, mountain,

even "figure" itself—and all with deliberately sexual con-
notations. It is almost as though Rilke were consciously and
specifically reminding his readers that these are always and
above all sexual symbols in his poetry (and, indeed, in all
poetry); that, for example, the tower in the ninth of the
Duino Elegies and the tree in the first of the *Sonnets to
Orpheus* are fundamentally sexual, whatever else they may
also be.

Another noticeable feature of these love poems is their
remarkable combination of great passion and gentle care.
It is as if Rilke's poetic gestures were both wildly and softly
caressing. To put it another way, Rilke's unique joining of
the masculine and the feminine, discussed earlier in his letters, is here profoundly portrayed in his poetry.

And yet, to be fair, one must say that Rilke's own love
relationships had something questionable in them at times.
But is not that true of us all? Still, rightly or wrongly, we
expect one who can articulate so beautiful and profound a
vision somehow to live it a bit better than the rest of us. Especially a poet like Rilke, who concluded a description of
an ancient fragment of sculpture by saying, "You must
change your life" ["Du mußt dein Leben ändern"]. The relation between art and living is complex, especially in the
modern period of aestheticism. I can only say here that my
own sense of Rilke is that he was in no way an aesthete, nor
is his poetry. That precisely in this area of the sensual, as
in every other, he wanted art and life to connect, to transform each other. And that in his bearing this difficult task,
he left us something most precious and indispensable, in
spite of whatever questions might remain.

Finally, all of these poems were written by Rilke during
his thirties and forties, that is, during the period of his most
mature work. No youthful romantic effusions here. The
poems are not only deeply sensual, they are tough-minded
as well. They fully deserve to take their place alongside

Donne's great love poems. I only hope this presentation will help hasten that time. It should at least correct the long-standing impression, present in America and widespread in Europe, that Rilke's poetry is somewhat precious and even effeminate.

[I]

Auf einmal faßt die Rosenpflückerin
die volle Knospe seines Lebensgliedes,
und an dem Schreck des Unterschiedes
schwinden die [linden] Gärten in ihr hin

[II]

Du hast mir, Sommer, der du plötzlich bist,
zum jähen Baum den Samen aufgezogen.
(Innen Geräumige, fühl in dir den Bogen
der Nacht, in der er mündig ist.)
Nun hob er sich und wächst zum Firmament,
ein Spiegelbild das neben Bäumen steht.
O stürz ihn, daß er, umgedreht
in deinen Schooß, den Gegen-Himmel kennt,
in den er wirklich bäumt und wirklich ragt.
Gewagte Landschaft, wie sie Seherinnen
in Kugeln schauen. Jenes Innen
in das das Draußensein der Sterne jagt.
[Dort tagt der Tod, der draußen nächtig scheint.
Und dort sind alle, welche waren,
mit allen Künftigen vereint

RILKE'S POEMS ON LOVE

The Seven Phallic Poems

[I]

The rose-gatherer grasps suddenly
the full bud of his vitality,
and, at fright at the difference,
the gentle garden within her shrinks
October, 1915

[II]

Summer, which you so suddenly are, you're
drawing my seed up into an abrupt tree.
(Inner spaciousness, feel in yourself the lee
of night in which it is mature.)
Now to the firmament it rose and grew,
a mirror-image resembling a tree.
O fell it, that, having turned unerringly
in your womb, it knows the counter-heaven anew,
in which it really towers and really races.
Daring landscape, such as an inner-seer
beholds in a crystal ball. That innerness here
in which the being-outside of stars chases.
There dawns death which shines outside like night.
And there, joined with all futures,
are all who once were, the finite,

und Scharen scharen sich um Scharen
wie es der Engel meint.]

[III]

Mit unsern Blicken schließen wir den Kreis,
daß weiß in ihm [die] wirre Spannung schmölze.
Schon richtet dein unwissendes Geheiß
die Säule auf in meinem Schamgehölze.

Von dir gestiftet steht des Gottes Bild
am leisen Kreuzweg unter meinem Kleide;
mein ganzer Körper heißt nach ihm. Wir beide
sind wie ein Gau darin sein Zauber gilt.

Doch Hain zu sein und Himmel um die Herme
das ist an dir. Gieb nach. Damit
der freie Gott inmitten seiner Schwärme
aus der entzückt zerstörten Säule tritt.

[IV]

Schwindende, du kennst die Türme nicht.
Doch nun sollst du einen Turm gewahren
mit dem wunderbaren
Raum in dir. Verschließ dein Angesicht
Aufgerichtet hast du ihn
ahnungslos mit Blick und Wink und Wendung.
Plötzlich starrt er von Vollendung,
und ich, Seliger, darf ihn beziehn.
Ach wie bin ich eng darin.
Schmeichle mir, zur Kuppel auszutreten:
um in deine weichen Nächte hin
mit dem Schwung schooßblendender Raketen
mehr Gefühl zu schleudern, als ich bin.

[V]

Wie hat uns der zu weite Raum verdünnt.
Plötzlich besinnen sich die Überflüsse.

crowds crowded round crowds for sure,
as the angel intends it outright.

October, 1915

[III]

We close a circle by means of our gazes,
and in it the tangled tension fuses white.
Already your unwitting command raises
the column in my genital-woodsite.

Granted by you, the image of the god stands
at the gentle crossroads under my clothes;
my whole body is named after him. We both
matter like a province in his magic lands.

Yet yours is to be grove and heaven around
the Hermean pillar. Yield. Thereby freedom
for the god along with his hounds,
withdrawn from the delightfully ravaged column.

October, 1915

[IV]

You don't know towers, with your diffidence.
Yet now you'll become aware
of a tower in that wonderful rare
space in you. Hide your countenance.
You've erected it unsuspectingly,
by turn and glance and indirection,
and I, blissful one, am allowed entry.
Ah, how in there I am so tight.
Coax me to come forth to the summit:
so as to fling into your soft night,
with the soaring of a womb-dazzling rocket,
more feeling than I am quite.

October, 1915

[V]

How the too ample space has weakened you and me.
Superfluity recollects itself suddenly.

47

Nun sickert durch das stille Sieb der Küsse
des bittren Wesens Alsem und Absynth.

Was sind wir viel, aus meinem Körper hebt
ein neuer Baum die überfüllte Krone
und ragt nach dir: denn sieh, was ist er ohne
den Sommer, der in deinem Schooße schwebt.
Bist du's bin ich's, den wir so sehr beglücken?
Wer sagt es, da wir schwinden. Vielleicht steht
im Zimmer eine Säule aus Entzücken,
die Wölbung trägt und langsamer vergeht.

[VI]

Wem sind wir nah? Dem Tode oder dem,
was noch nicht ist? Was wäre Lehm an Lehm,
formte der Gott nicht fühlend die Figur,
die zwischen uns erwächst. Begreife nur:
das ist mein Körper, welcher aufersteht.
Nun hilf ihm leise aus dem heißen Grabe
in jenen Himmel, den ich in dir habe:
daß kühn aus ihm das Überleben geht.
Du junger Ort der tiefen Himmelfahrt.
Du dunkle Luft voll sommerlicher Pollen.
Wenn ihre tausend Geister in dir tollen,
wird meine steife Leiche wieder zart.

[VII]

Wie rief ich dich. Das sind die stummen Rufe,
die in mir süß geworden sind.
Nun stoß ich in dich Stufe ein um Stufe
und heiter steigt mein Samen wie ein Kind.
Du Urgebirg der Lust: auf einmal springt
er atemlos zu deinem innern Grate.
O gieb dich hin, zu fühlen wie er nahte;
denn du wirst stürzen, wenn er oben winkt.

Now wormwood and absinthe trickle through silent
sieves of kisses of bitter essence.

How much we are—from my body
a new tree raises its abundant crown
and mounts toward you: but what's it to be
without the summer which hovers in your womb.
Are you, am I, the one each so greatly delights?
Who can say, while we dwindle. Perhaps a column
of rapture stands in the chamber room,
sustains the vault, and more slowly subsides.

November, 1915

[VI]

To what are we near? To death, or that display
which is not yet? For what would be clay to clay
had not the god feelingly formed the figure
which grows between us. But understand for sure:
this is my body which is resurrected.
Now gently deliver it from the burning grave
into that heaven which in you I crave:
that from it survival be boldly effected.
You young place of ascension deep.
You dark breeze of summery pollen.
When its thousand spirits romp madly all in
you, my stiff corpse again grows soft asleep.

November, 1915

[VII]

How I called you. This is the mute call
which within me has grown sweet awhile.
Now step after step into you I thrust all
and my semen climbs gladly like a child.
You primal peak of pleasure: suddenly well-nigh
breathless it leaps to your inner ridge.
O surrender yourself to feeling its pilgrimage;
for you'll be hurled down when it waves on high.

November, 1915

GRIECHISCHES LIEBESGESPRÄCH

Was ich schon früh als Geliebter erlernte
seh ich dich zürnend, Geliebte, erlernen;
damals war es dir das Entfernte,
jetzt steht in allen Sternen dein Los.

Um deine Brüste werden wir streiten:
seit sie wie glühend beschienen reifen,
wollen auch deine Hände nach ihnen
greifen und sich Freude bereiten.

DIE LIEBENDEN

Sieh, wie sie zu einander erwachsen:
in ihren Adern wird alles Geist.
Ihre Gestalten beben wie Achsen,
um die es heiß und hinreißend kreist.
Dürstende, und sie bekommen zu trinken,
Wache und sieh: sie bekommen zu sehn.
Laß sie ineinander sinken,
um einander zu überstehn.

Sag weißt du Liebesnächte? Treiben nicht
auf deinem Blut Kelchblätter weicher Worte?
Sind nicht an deinem lieben Leibe Orte,
die sich entsinnen wie ein Angesicht?

Other Love Poems

GREEK LOVE-TALK

What I, as one loved, already early learned,
I see you, beloved, learning angrily;
then for you it distantly sojourned,
now your destiny stands in all the stars.

Over your breasts we will together contend:
since as glowingly shining they've ripened,
so also your hands desire to touch them
and their own pleasure superintend.

Fall, 1907, or Spring, 1908

THE LOVERS

See how in their veins all becomes spirit:
into each other they mature and grow.
Like axles, their forms tremblingly orbit,
round which it whirls, bewitching and aglow.
Thirsters, and they receive drink,
watchers, and see: they receive sight.
Let them into one another sink
so as to endure each other outright.

Summer, 1908

You declare you know love's nights? Have not bud
and sepal of soft words blossomed in your blood?
Are there not on your beloved body places
which recollect like open faces?

Summer, 1909

. . . . diese weichen
Nächte halten mich wie ihresgleichen
und ich liege ohne Lieblingin.

Bilden die Nächte sich nicht aus dem schmerzlichen Raum
aller der Arme die jäh ein Geliebter verließ.
Ewige Liebende, die überstehn will: ergieß
dich als Quelle, schließ dich als Lorbeerbaum.

Welche Wiesen duften deine Hände?
Fühlst du wie auf deine Widerstände
stärker sich der Duft von draußen stützt.
Drüber stehn die Sterne schon in Bildern.
Gieb mir, Liebe, deinen Mund zu mildern;
ach, dein ganzes Haar ist unbenützt.

Sieh, ich will dich mit dir selbst umgeben
und die welkende Erwartung heben
von dem Rande deiner Augenbraun;
wie mit lauter Liderinnenseiten
will ich dir mit meinen Zärtlichkeiten
alle Stellen schließen, welche schaun.

Auch noch das Entzücken wie ein Ding
auszusagen

. . . . these soft
nights hold me like themselves aloft
and I lie without a lover.

Summer, 1909

Are not the nights fashioned from the sorrowful
space of all the open arms a lover suddenly lost.
Eternal lover, who desires to endure: exhaust
yourself like a spring, enclose yourself like a laurel.

Summer, 1909

What fields are fragrant as your hands?
You feel how external fragrance stands
upon your stronger resistance.
Stars stand in images above.
Give me your mouth to soften, love;
ah, your hair is all in idleness.

See, I want to surround you with yourself
and the faded expectation lift
from the edges of your eyebrows;
I want, as with inner eyelids sheer,
to close for you all places which appear
by my tender caresses now.

Summer, 1909

Also to affirm even rapture
like a thing

Summer, 1909

Und der Letzte geht vielleicht vorüber
und erkennt mich nicht obzwar ich brenn.
Ach die Bäume hängen glühend über
und ich fühle keinen Fühlenden.

So wie eine Türe, die nicht zubleibt,
geht im Schlaf mir immer wieder stöhnend
die Umarmung auf. Oh wehe Nächte.

Draußen wird der Garten weich im Mondschein
und die Blüten trüben mir das Fenster
und die Nachtigall ist nicht vergebens.

Dies ist das schweigende Steigen der Phallen

Wie man rasch Erwachsenden die Zöpfe
anders ordnet, legt man das Gelock
dieser selig grünenden Geschöpfe
sorgsam anders um Gestalt und Pflock.

Wie sie wachsen, wie sie sich befreien,
unter Sommerschürzen langsam prall;
ach, was sich an Mädchen spannt in zweien
neuen Brüsten, spannt sie überall.

An der sonngewohnten Straße, in dem
hohlen halben Baumstamm, der seit lange
Trog ward, eine Oberfläche Wasser

WOMAN'S LAMENT I
And the last perhaps will not return
and knows me not although I burn.
Ah the trees overhang glowingly
and I feel no one feeling me.
Early 1911

WOMAN'S LAMENT II
So like a door which won't stay closed,
my moaning embraces open in sleep
again and again. Oh nights of woe.

Outside grows the garden gently in the moonlight
and the blossoms dim my window
and the nightingale is not in vain.
Early 1911

This is the mute-mouthed mounting of the phalli
February, 1922

Like the pigtails of quickly grown-up girls
one braids differently, one sets the curls
of these blissfully greening creatures with care
and differently round shape and pin there.

How they are freeing themselves, how they grow,
under summer pinafores stretching so slow;
ah, what to a maiden rouses two new breasts,
she arouses over all the rest.
End of 1923

By the sun-surrounded road, within the
hollow open tree trunk which for long has
been a trough in which a film of water

55

in sich leis erneuernd, still' ich meinen
Durst: des Wassers Heiterkeit und Herkunft
in mich nehmend durch die Handgelenke.
Trinken schiene mir zu viel, zu deutlich;
aber diese wartende Gebärde
holt mir helles Wasser ins Bewußtsein.

Also, kämst du, braucht ich, mich zu stillen,
nur ein leichtes Anruhn meiner Hände,
sei's an deiner Schulter junge Rundung,
sei es an den Andrang deiner Brüste.

(Da ich dir schrieb, sprang Saft
auf in der männlichen Blume,
die meinem Menschentume
reich ist und rätselhaft.

Fühlst du, da du mich liest,
ferne Zärtliche, welche
Süße im weiblichen Kelche
willig zusammenfließt?)

is renewed so softly, there I still my
thirst: the clearness and epiphany of
water enters me across and through my wrists.
Drinking would seem too much, too plain, to me;
but this expectant gesture draws
the shining water into my consciousness.

Therefore, if you came, I'd need, to still me,
just a gentle resting of my hands,
be it on the youthful rounding of your shoulder,
be it on the pressure of your breasts.

June, 1924

(Since I wrote you, sap sprang free
in the masculine blooming,
which is rich and puzzling
to my very humanity.

Do you feel, distant dear miss,
since you are reading me,
what sweetness fuses willingly
in the feminine chalice?)

July, 1924

IV. *Poems on Other Difficulties*

INTRODUCTION

——

It is time—who can doubt it?—to reread Rilke. Or, rather, to read the later Rilke, the post–*Sonnets to Orpheus* Rilke.

The standard view of Rilke goes something like this. He began as a bit of a sticky late Romantic. His vision was expanded by Nietzsche, and by his experiences in Russia with Lou Andreas-Salomé and at the artists' colony at Worpswede. His poetry was refined into a mature work in the double fire of disciplined technique under Rodin (*New Poems*) and cathartic psychological exploration (*The Notebooks of Malte Laurids Brigge*). Then the first few of the *Duino Elegies* came to him in 1912 and he began the long, arduous stuggle to achieve what he was convinced would be his great poetic work. Not until ten years later, in the "great giving" of February, 1922, did he accomplish that task. Not only did he finish the ten *Duino Elegies,* but the fifty-five *Sonnets to Orpheus* and a number of other poems as well. It was indeed the most remarkable of Rilke's great creative bursts, and perhaps the most remarkable in literature. In three weeks, he wrote, by my count, more than 1,600 lines of poetry, plus a major essay—"The Young Workman's Letter"—and his usual quota of personal letters. The traditional opinion is that the *Duino Elegies* is indeed his masterpiece, in whose wake also came, unexpectedly, the important though somewhat slighter *Sonnets to Orpheus.* A variation on this view is that the *Sonnets* surpass to some extent the

Elegies. Both versions, however, assume that Rilke's last years, after the great giving, produced nothing to equal or surpass the *Elegies* and *Sonnets*. Rilke himself, no doubt remembering the long struggle to write the *Elegies,* encouraged these views. In fact, it took him a while to see that the *Sonnets* were more than merely fragments in the wake of the *Elegies.*

Forgotten in all of this, however, is the fact that in the nearly five years after the great giving, Rilke wrote two hundred poems and fragments, many of them major in length, almost all of them, whether long or short, of great importance. The distinguished critic Beda Allemann, almost alone among commentators, has made a significant case for the view that these last poems are, in fact, Rilke's supreme achievement. Even Yeats, with his remarkable later poetry, does not exceed Rilke's last work.

Encomiums may be useful to catch one's attention. Exhibits are required to make the point. Leishman's translations of Rilke's last poetry (included in Rilke, *Poems 1906 to 1926* [New York: New Directions, 1957]) are good. We are forever in his debt. But one feels he hurried. And these two hundred last poems are buried in the seven hundred poems of that volume. A chest of jewels is impressive. But one can hardly thereby appreciate the quality of individual stones. Here, then, are a few selected flawless gems, in what I trust are fresh, though hardly faultless, translations. All but a couple of the poems have appeared in translation only once before (in Leishman's volume).

I begin with a poem just before the great giving. It is followed by one from that incredible explosion of creativity itself. The other poems and fragments come from the last three years of Rilke's life. In fact, two-thirds of them come from 1924 alone, two years before his death. They portray the perennial struggles and themes and difficulties with which his poetry deals: death, night, things, gods, silence and words (and song and music), growing, transformation,

the earth, fire, dance, etc.—though with even greater sub-
tlety, density, and depth than before. A new plateau is
reached here, one that discloses paths and possibilities more
provocative even than the earlier works, and certainly at
least as relevant, to use a word currently in vogue, as when
they were written. For who would deny that transformation
is the primal task with which man today is faced?

My choices were made for various reasons: they are some
of my favorites, they are a representative cross section, certain ones reflect particular concerns of mine at the time I
was working on the translations (e.g., music, night), one
was discussed at length by Allemann, and so on. All of
them, as indeed all of Rilke's work, deal with the fundamental difficulty of living-dying, in all its multitudinous manifestations. Rilke, who began so far ahead of most of us and
began so far behind most beginning poets, was still beginning at the end.

nonsense words

Oh sage, Dichter, was du tust?
                              —Ich rühme.
Aber das Tödliche und Ungetüme,
wie hältst du's aus, wie nimmst du's hin?
                              —Ich rühme.
Aber das Namenlose, Anonyme,
wie rufst du's, Dichter, dennoch an?
                              —Ich rühme.
Woher dein Recht, in jeglichem Kostume,
in jeder Maske wahr zu sein?
                              —Ich rühme.
Und daß das Stille und das Ungestüme
wie Stern und Sturm dich kennen?
                              :—weil ich rühme.

RILKE'S POEMS ON
OTHER DIFFICULTIES

The Poet Speaks of Praising

Oh speak, poet, what do you do?
                          —I praise.
But the monstrosities and the murderous days,
how do you endure them, how do you take them?
                          —I praise.
But the anonymous, the nameless grays,
how, poet, do you still invoke them?
                          —I praise.
What right have you, in all displays,
in very mask, to be genuine?
                          —I praise.
And that the stillness and the turbulent sprays
know you like star and storm?
                          :—since I praise.

December, 1921

Wartet . . . , das schmeckt . . . Schon ists auf der Flucht.
. . . Wenig Musik nur, ein Stampfen, ein Summen—:
Mädchen, ihr warmen, Mädchen, ihr stummen,
tanzt den Geschmack der erfahrenen Frucht!

Tanzt die Orange. Wer kann sie vergessen,
wie sie, ertrinkend in sich, sich wehrt
wider ihr Süßsein. Ihr habt sie besessen.
Sie hat sich köstlich zu euch bekehrt.

Tanzt die Orange. Die wärmere Landschaft,
werft sie aus euch, daß die reife erstrahle
in Lüften der Heimat! Erglühte, enthüllt

Düfte um Düfte. Schafft die Verwandtschaft
mit der reinen, sich weigernden Schale,
mit dem Saft, der die Glückliche füllt!

The Poet Praises

Wait . . . , this tastes good . . . Already it's in pursuit.
. . . Only a little music, a stamping, a hum—:
Maidens, you warm ones, maidens, you mute and dumb,
dance the taste of the experienced fruit!

Dance the orange. Who can forget it,
how, drowning in itself, it grew
against its being-sweet. You have possessed it.
It has been deliciously converted into you.

Dance the orange. The warmer landscape,
throw it from you, that the ripeness shine
in the breezes of home! Aglow, disclosing

aroma on aroma. Create the kin-shape
with the pure, the reluctant rine,
with the juice which fills the fortunate thing!

Die Sonette an Orpheus, *I, 15*
February, 1922

Leben und *Tod*: sie sind im Kerne Eins.
Wer sich begreift aus seinem eignen Stamme,
der preßt sich selber zu dem Tropfen Weins
und wirft sich selber in die reinste Flamme.

Spiele die Tode, die einzelnen, rasch und du
                         [wirst sie erkennen
wie sie sich schließt die unendliche Strömung der Sterne;

. . . . Wandlung
Hymnen im Innern, Tanz vor der Arche,
Aufruhr und Aufzug im reifenden Wein

Starker Stern, der nicht den Beistand braucht,
den die Nacht den andern mag gewähren,
die erst dunkeln muß, daß sie sich klären.
Stern, der schon vollendet, untertaucht,

The Poems Praise

Life and *death*: they are one, at core entwined.
Who understands himself from his own strain
presses himself into a drop of wine
and throws himself into the purest flame.
                                        Christmas, 1922

Play the deaths, the single ones, quickly and you
                                        [will recognize it
as it closes on itself the unending stream of stars;
                                        End of 1923

. . . . Transformation
Hymns in innerness, dance before the ark,
uproar and parade in the ripening vine
                                        December, 1923

Strong star, which needs not the help which
night might grant differently to those for which
it must first be dark for them to become clear.
Star already achieved, disappear

wenn Gestirne ihren Gang beginnen
durch die langsam aufgetane Nacht.
Großer Stern der Liebes-Priesterinnen,
der, von eigenem Gefühl entfacht,

bis zuletzt verklärt und nie verkohlend,
niedersinkt, wohin die Sonne sank:
tausendfachen Aufgang überholend
mit dem reinen Untergang.

Schweigen. Wer inniger schwieg,
rührt an die Wurzeln der Rede.
Einmal wird ihm dann jede
erwachsene Silbe zum Sieg:

über das, was im Schweigen nich schweigt,
über das höhnische Böse;
daß es sich spurlos löse,
ward ihm das Wort gezeigt.

Wandle Staubgefäß um Staubgefäß,
fülle deine innerliche Rose

Götter schreiten vielleicht   immer im gleichen Gewähren,
    wo unser Himmel beginnt;
wie in Gedanken erreicht   unsere schwereren Ähren,
    sanft sie wendend, ihr Wind.

when constellations begin their courses
through the slowly disclosed night.
Great star of love's-priestesses,
which feeling kindles from its own right,

till at last radiant and never charred,
it sinks down where the sun sank westward:
surpassing thousandfold ascent
with the pure descent.

January, 1924

Being-silent. Who keeps innerly
silent, touches the roots of speech.
Once for him becomes then each
growing syllable victory:

over what in silence keeps not silent,
over the insulting evil;
to dissolve itself to nil,
was the word to him made evident.

January, 1924

Transform stamen on stamen,
fill your interior rose

February, 1924

Gods perhaps are still striding along,   always with the
                                            [very same warrant,
    there where our heavens commence;
as in thoughts their wind reaches ere long   our ears of
                                            [grain so luxuriant,
    gently turning them thence.

Rilke on Love and Other Difficulties

Wer sie zu fühlen vergaß,   leistet nicht ganz die
                                                    [Verzichtung:
        dennoch haben sie teil.
Schweigsam, einfach und heil   legt sich an seine
                                                    [Errichtung
        plötzlich ihr anderes Maß.

Wir sollen nicht wissen, warum
dieses und jenes uns meistert;
wirkliches Leben ist stumm,
nur, daß es uns begeistert,

macht uns mit ihm vertraut

Heitres Geschenk von den kältern
Bergen
versucht in den Juni den Sprung;
blinkend in Back und Behältern
drängt sich Erneuerung.

Überall unter verstaubten
Büschen
lebendiger Wasser Gang;
und wie sie selig behaupten,
Gehn sei Gesang.

Alles ist Spiel, aber Spiele . . .

Who forgot to feel them performs   not fully the
                             [relinquishment himself:
    nevertheless they have a share.
Silent, whole, and solitaire,   their different measure
                             [suddenly adheres itself
    to its erected forms.

February, 1924

We are not to know why
this and that masters us;
real life makes no reply,
only that it enraptures us

makes us familiar with it
May, 1924

Cheerful gift from the chillier
mountains
attempts the leap into June;
renewal crowds so glittery
in brook and lagoon.

Everywhere under dust-stained
shrubs
more lively waters go along;
and as they happily maintain,
going is song.

June, 1924

Everything is play, and yet plays . . .
July, 1924

MAGIE

Aus unbeschreiblicher Verwandlung stammen
solche Gebilde—: Fühl! und glaub!
Wir leidens oft: zu Asche werden Flammen;
doch, in der Kunst: zur Flamme wird der Staub.

Hier ist Magie. In das Bereich des Zaubers
scheint das gemeine Wort hinaufgestuft . . .
und ist doch wirklich wie der Ruf des Taubers,
der nach der unsichtbaren Taube ruft.

Nach so langer Erfahrung sei "Haus,"
"Baum" oder "Brücke" anders gewagt.
Immer dem Schicksal eingesagt,
sag es sich endlich aus.

Daß wir das tägliche Wesen entwirrn,
das jeder anders erfuhr,
machen wir uns ein Nachtgestirn
aus der gewußten Figur.

Was sich uns reicht mit dem Sternenlicht,
was sich uns reicht,
faß es wie Welt in dein Angesicht,
nimm es nicht leicht.

Zeige der Nacht, daß du still empfingst,
was sie gebracht.
Erst wenn du ganz zu ihr übergingst,
kennt dich die Nacht.

MAGIC

From indescribable transformation flash
such creations—: Feel! and trust!
We suffer it often: flames become ash;
yet, in art: flames come from dust.

Here is magic. In the realm of a spell
the common word seems lifted up above . . .
and yet is really like the call of the male
who calls for the invisible female dove.

August, 1924

After such long experience let "house,"
"tree," or "bridge" be dared differently.
Always whispered to destiny,
finally and at last say it out.

To untangle daily creation,
which all differently endure,
we make ourselves a constellation
out of the known figure.

August, 1924

That which offers itself to us with starlight,
that which offers itself to us,
hold it like world in your face with might,
take it seriously.

Show night that you received silently
what it bestowed on you.
Not until you go over to it entirely
will night know you.

August, 1924

Die Quitten gilben aus dem grauen Flaume

AUS DEM UMKREIS: NÄCHTE

Nacht. Oh du in Tiefe gelöstes
Gesicht an meinem Gesicht.
Du, meines staunenden Anschauns größtes
Übergewicht.

Nacht, in meinem Blicke erschauernd,
aber in sich so fest;
unerschöpfliche Schöpfung, dauernd
über dem Erdenrest;

voll von jungen Gestirnen, die Feuer
aus der Flucht ihres Saums
schleudern ins lautlose Abenteuer
des Zwischenraums:

wie, durch dein bloßes Dasein, erschein ich,
Übertrefferin, klein—;
doch, mit der dunkelen Erde einig,
wag ich es, in dir zu sein.

SCHWERKRAFT

Mitte, wie du aus allen
dich ziehst, auch noch aus Fliegenden dich
widergewinnst, Mitte, du Stärkste.

Stehender: wie ein Trank den Durst
durchstürzt ihn die Schwerkraft.

Doch aus dem Schlafenden fällt,
wie aus lagernder Wolke,
reichlicher Regen der Schwere.

The quinces yellow from their gray fluff
                    September, 1924

FROM THE CYCLE: NIGHTS
Night. Oh you in depths dissolving,
face against my own.
You, my astonished staring's
greatest millstone.

Night, in my glance shuddering,
but in itself so strong;
inexhaustible creation, enduring
beyond the earth so long;

        full of young constellations, which hurl
fire from the flight of their border-place
into the inaudible adventure
of interspace:

though by you naked being,
surpasser, I appear tiny—;
still, one with the darkening
earth, I dare in you to be.
                    October, 1924

FORCE OF GRAVITY
Center, how you draw yourself out
from all things, how you also reclaim yourself
from flying things, center, you strongest.

Stander: like a drink through thirst
hurtles the force of gravity through him.

Yet from the sleeper falls,
as from a stored up cloud,
abundant rain of force.
                    October, 1924

77

MAUSOLEUM

Königsherz. Kern eines hohen
Herrscherbaums. Balsamfrucht.
Goldene Herznuß. Urnen-Mohn
mitten im Mittelbau,
(wo der Widerhall abspringt,
wie ein Splitter der Stille,
wenn du dich rührst,
weil es dir scheint,
daß deine vorige
Haltung zu laut war . . .)
Völkern entzogenes,
sterngesinnt,
im unsichtbaren Kreisen
kreisendes Königsherz.

Wo ist, wohin,
jenes der leichten
Lieblingin?
:   Lächeln, von außen,
auf die zögernde Rundung
heiterer Früchte gelegt;
oder der Motte, vielleicht,
Kostbarkeit, Florflügel, Fühler . . .

Wo aber, wo, das sie sang,
das sie in Eins sang,
das Dichterherz?
:   Wind,
unsichtbar,
Windinnres.

Irgendwo blüht die Blume des Abschieds und streut
immerfort Blütenstaub, den wir atmen, herüber;
auch noch im kommendsten Wind atmen wir Abschied.

MAUSOLEUM

King's-heart. Kernel of a lofty
lordly-tree. Balsam-fruit.
Golden heart-nut. Poppy of urns
in the middle of the middle-building
(where the reverberation cracks off
like a splinter of stillness
when you bestir yourself,
since it seems to you
that your previous
bearing was too loud . . .),
nation evaded,
star-minded,
in invisible circle
circling king's-heart.

Where, whither is
the nimble lover's
one?
:   Smile, from without,
placed onto the hesitant
roundness of cheerful fruits;
or for the moth, perhaps,
costliness, gauze-wing, feeler . . .

Where, but where, that which sang her,
that which sang her into one,
the poet's-heart?
:   Wind,
invisible,
wind-innerness.

October, 1924

Somewhere blooms the blossom of parting and bestrews
evermore over us pollen which we breathe:
even in the most-coming wind we breathe parting.

October, 1924

Aufgedeckter das Land: auf allen Wegen ist Heimkehr,
durch den gelockerten Baum sieht man das Haus, wie
[es währt.
Himmel entfernt sich von uns. Wärmt nun, oh Herzen,
[die Erde,
daß sie uns innig gehört in dem verlassenen Raum.

Gieb mir, oh Erde, den reinen
Thon für den Tränenkrug;
mein Wesen, ergieße das Weinen,
das sich in dir verschlug.

Daß sich Verhaltenes löse
in das gefügte Gefäß.
Nur das Nirgends ist böse,
alles Sein ist gemäß.

Ach, nicht getrennt sein,
nicht durch so wenig Wandung
ausgeschlossen vom Sternen-Maß.
Innres, was ists?
Wenn nicht gesteigerter Himmel,
durchworfen mit Vögeln und tief
von Winden der Heimkehr.

Die Stimmen warnten mich, da hielt ich ein

More uncovered the land: on every way is hometurning,
through the relaxed tree one sees the house as it lasts.
Sky withdraws itself from us. Now warm, oh hearts,
                                                    [the earth,
so that it belongs intimately to us in the abandoned space.
October, 1924

Give me, oh earth, pure unmingling
clay for the jug of tears;
my essence, pour forth the weeping
which is lost in you here.

   In the well-made vessel,
that restraint dissolves itself.
Only the nowhere is evil,
all being suits itself.
October, 1924

Ah, not being sundered,
not through such a little partition
excluded from the star-measure.
Innerness, what is it?
If not heightened sky,
scattered through with birds and deep
from winds of hometurning.
Summer, 1925

The voices warned me so I desisted
July, 1925

Jetzt wär es Zeit, daß Götter träten aus
bewohnten Dingen . . .
Und daß sie jede Wand in meinem Haus
umschlügen. Neue Seite. Nur der Wind,
den solches Blatt in Wenden würfe, reichte hin,
die Luft, wie eine Scholle, umzuschaufeln:
ein neues Atemfeld. Oh Götter, Götter!
Ihr Oftgekommnen, Schläfer in den Dingen,
die heiter aufstehn, die sich an den Brunnen,
die wir vermuten, Hals und Antlitz waschen
und die ihr Ausgeruhtsein leicht hinzutun
zu dem, was voll scheint, unserm vollen Leben.
Noch einmal sei es euer Morgen, Götter.
Wir wiederholen. Ihr allein seid Ursprung.
Die Welt steht auf mit euch, und Anfang glänzt
an allen Bruchstelln unseres Mißlingens . . .

GONG

Nicht mehr für Ohren . . . : Klang,
der, wie ein tieferes Ohr,
uns, scheinbar Hörende, hört.
Umkehr der Räume. Entwurf
innerer Welten im Frein . . . ,
Tempel vor ihrer Geburt,
Lösung, gesättigt mit schwer
löslichen Göttern . . . : Gong!

Summe des Schweigenden, das
sich zu sich selber bekennt,
brausende Einkehr in sich
dessen, das an sich verstummt,
Dauer, aus Ablauf gepreßt,
um-gegossener Stern . . . : Gong!

Now it would be time that gods should step out
from inhabited things . . .
And that they should knock down every wall
in my house. New sides. Only the wind
which such a leaf would throw in turning would suffice
to shovel the air over like sod:
a new breath-field. Oh gods, gods!
You often-comers, sleepers in things,
who arise brightly, who, at the spring
we conjecture, wash face and neck,
and who lightly add their being-reposed
to that which seems full, our full life.
Once more be it your morning, gods.
We repeat. You alone are origin.
The world gets up with you, and beginning glistens
on all the breaking-places of our failure . . .

October, 1925

GONG

No more for ears . . . : tone
which, like a deeper ear,
hears us, seeming hearers.
Turning-back of spaces. Sketch
of inner worlds out in the open . . . ,
temples before their birth,
solution saturated with heavy
soluble gods . . . : gong!

Sum of silencing, which
acknowledges itself to itself,
stormy entrance into itself
of that which becomes mute on its own,
enduring squeezed out of elapsing,
re-cast star . . . : gong!

Du, die man niemals vergißt,
die sich gebar im Verlust,
nichtmehr begriffenes Fest,
Wein an unsichtbarem Mund,
Sturm in der Säule, die trägt,
Wanderers Sturz in den Weg,
unser, an Alles, Verrat . . . : Gong!

Aber versuchtest du dies: Hand in der Hand mir zu sein
wie im Weinglas der Wein Wein ist.
Versuchtest du dies.

MUSIK

Die, welche schläft . . . . Um bei dem reinen Wecken
so wach zu sein, daß wir zu Schläfern werden
von ihrem Wachsein überholt . . . . Oh Schrecken!
Schlag an die Erde: sie klingt stumpf und erden,
gedämpft und eingehüllt von unsern Zwecken.
Schlag an den Stern: er wird sich dir entdecken!

Schlag an den Stern: die unsichtbaren Zahlen
erfüllen sich; Vermögen der Atome
vermehren sich im Raume. Töne strahlen.
Und was hier Ohr ist ihrem vollen Strome,
ist irgendwo auch Auge: diese Dome
wölben sich irgendwo im Idealen.

Irgendwo *steht* Musik, wie irgendwo
dies Licht in Ohren fällt als fernes Klingen . . . .
Für unsre Sinne einzig scheint das so
getrennt . . . Und zwischen dem und jenem Schwingen
schwingt namenlos der Überfluß. . . . Was floh

You, whom one never forgets,
who gave birth to itself in loss,
no-more understood festival,
wine at invisible mouth,
storm in the column that supports,
wanderer's fall in the way,
our treason toward all . . . : gong!

November, 1925

If you'd attempt this, however: hand in hand to be mine,
as the wine in the wineglass is wine.
If you'd attempt this.

November, 1925

MUSIC

She who sleeps . . . . To be so very awake,
near pure waking, that we into sleepers grow,
surpassed by its being-awake . . . . Oh quake!
Pound on the earth: dull and earthen its echo,
deadened and muffled by what we undertake.
Pound on the star: 'twill disclose itself for your sake!

Pound on the star: invisible number signs
are realized; the capacities of an atom
are multiplying in space. The tone shines.
And what here is ear to its fulsome
stream, is also somewhere eye: this dome
arches itself somewhere in designs.

Somewhere *stands* music, just as somewhere this light
falls on ears as a distant resonating . . . .
Only for our senses does that seem quite
so sundered . . . And between this and that vibrating
vibrates abundance namelessly. . . . What takes flight

in Früchte? Giebt im Kreis des Schmeckens
uns seinen Wert? Was teilt ein Duft uns mit?
(Was wir auch tun, mit einem jeden Schritt
verwischen wir die Grenzen des Entdeckens.)

❈   ❈   ❈

Musik: du Wasser unsres Brunnenbeckens,
Du Strahl der fällt, du Ton der spiegelt, du
selig Erwachte unterm Griff des Weckens,
du durch den Zufluß rein ergänzte Ruh,
Du mehr als wir . . . , von jeglichem Wozu
befreit . . . .

Bedenkst du's auch, daß eine blinde Welt
uns rings umgiebt? Wir einzig gegenüber,
wir Becherspiel, in das die Kugel fällt

und alles Nie-gehörende sei Dein!

Komm du, du letzter, den ich anerkenne,
heilloser Schmerz im leiblichen Geweb:
wie ich im Geiste brannte, sieh, ich brenne
in dir; das Holz hat lange widerstrebt,
der Flamme, die du loderst, zuzustimmen,
nun aber nähr' ich dich und brenn in dir.
Mein hiesig Mildsein wird in deinem Grimmen
ein Grimm der Hölle nicht von hier.
Ganz rein, ganz planlos frei von Zukunft stieg

into fruits? Gives us, in the circling intake
of tasting, its worth? What to us communicates
aroma? (Whate'er we do, we obliterate
the borders of disclosure with each step we take.)

❀   ❀   ❀

Music: you water of our fountain-basin,
You shining ray which falls, you sound which reflects, you
blissful awakener in the grasp of waking,
you rest through inflow purely restored,
You more than us . . . , from every wherefore
freed . . . .

December, 1925

Do you also ponder that we are all
surrounded by a blind world? We only face to face,
we gamecup, into which the ball falls

December, 1925 / January, 1926

and all never-belonging be yours!

September, 1926

Come you, you last one, whom I avow,
wretched pain in the corporeal weaving:
as I burned in spirit, see, I burn now
in you; the wood resisted receiving
for a long time the flame which in you glows,
now I feed you and burn in you as well.
In your rage my native being-mild grows
to a rage not from here but of hell.
Quite pure, quite planlessly free from future I

ich auf des Leidens wirren Scheiterhaufen,
so sicher nirgend Künftiges zu kaufen
um dieses Herz, darin der Vorrat schwieg.
Bin ich es noch, der da unkenntlich brennt?
Erinnerungen reiß ich nicht herein.
O Leben, Leben: Draußensein.
Und ich in Lohe. Niemand der mich kennt.

[Verzicht. Das ist nicht so wie Krankheit war
einst in der Kindheit. Aufschub. Vorwand um
größer zu werden. Alles rief und raunte.
Misch nicht in dieses was dich früh erstaunte]

climbed the tangled funeral pile of pain,
so sure nowhere to buy a future gain
for this heart, in which has grown silent the supply.
Is it still I who burns unrecognizably?
Memories I do not seize inside.
O life, life: being-outside.
And I in flame. No one who knows me.

Renunciation. That is not what illness
once was in childhood. Procrastination. Pretense for
growing bigger. Everything whispered and called.
Do not mix into this what early enthralled.

*Mid-December, 1926; last entry in last notebook,
less than two weeks before his death*

v. Blood-Remembering

RILKE HAD MUCH TO SAY about the difficulty of writing poetry. Not about the craft so much as about the inner life discipline. We have seen an example of that in the midst of his words on love. Another example is from his only full-scale novel, *The Notebooks of Malte Laurids Brigge* (completed in 1910). The novel is dialectically semi-autobiographical, but in the passage which shortly follows the young Malte is surely speaking directly with Rilke's own voice.

As is usual with Rilke, this passage deals not only with the writing of poetry but also, and by that very fact, with the living of life. It answers, in a profoundly positive way, the aesthetic fallacy of the expression theory of art (i.e., that art "expresses feelings"), and thereby the romantic notion held by many young people, artists and otherwise, that what one needs is only to experience things in order to know them. For Rilke, or for Malte, the progression is rather from feelings through experiences through memories through forgetting to what can be called, adapting Rilke's own words, *blood-remembering*. And from this blood-remembering comes poetry, and, for that matter, the wise old age which is like a ripe fruit just ready to fall.

Here, then, is Rilke on the difficulty of blood-remembering.

———

Ah! but verses amount to so little when one writes them young. One ought to wait and gather sense and sweetness a whole life long, and a long life if possible, and then, quite at the end, one might perhaps be able to write ten lines that were good. For verses are not, as people imagine, simply feelings (those one has early enough),—they are experiences. For the sake of a single verse, one must see many cities, men and things, one must know the animals, one must feel how the birds fly and know the gesture with which the little flowers open in the morning. One must be able to think back to roads in unknown regions, to unexpected meetings and to partings one had long seen coming; to days of childhood that are still unexplained, to parents whom one had to hurt when they brought one some joy and one did not grasp it (it was a joy for someone else); to childhood illnesses that so strangely begin with such a number of profound and grave transformations, to days in rooms withdrawn and quiet and to mornings by the sea, to the sea itself, to seas, to nights of travel that rushed along on high and flew with all the stars—and it is not yet enough if one may think of all this. One must have memories of many nights of love, none of which was like the others, of the screams of women in labor, and of light, white, sleeping women in childbed, closing again. But one must also have been beside the dying, must have sat beside the dead in the room with the open window and the fitful noises. And still it is not yet enough to have memories. One must be able to forget them when they are many and one must have the great patience to wait until they come again. For it is not yet the memories themselves. Not till they have turned to blood within us, to glance and gesture, nameless and no longer to be distinguished from ourselves—not till then can it happen that in a most rare hour the first word of a verse arises in their midst and goes forth from them.

VI. The Dragon-Princess

WHILE STILL ONLY IN HIS TWENTIES, Rilke penned what is for me the most affirmative passage of nonfiction prose I have ever come across. Characteristically, it is in a letter. And its affirmativeness comes in part precisely because of the tentativeness and ambiguity involved. Unambiguous affirmation is sentimentality. Rilke says "Perhaps." We heard him say earlier, "Perhaps man will then gradually, without noticing it, live along some distant day into the answer." Likewise, here again he says "Perhaps"—and in doing so speaks a word for us all.

———

To speak of solitude again, it becomes always clearer that this is at bottom not something that one can take or leave. We *are* solitary. We may delude ourselves and act as though this were not so. That is all. But how much better it is to realize that we are so, yes, even to begin by assuming it. We shall indeed turn dizzy then; for all points upon which our eye has been accustomed to rest are taken from us, there is nothing near any more and everything far is infinitely far. A person removed from his own room, almost without preparation and transition, and set upon the height of a great mountain range, would feel something of the sort: an unparalleled insecurity, an abandonment to something inexpressible would almost annihilate him. He would think himself falling or hurled out into space, or exploded into a thousand pieces: what a monstrous lie his brain would have to invent to catch up with and explain the state of his senses!

So for him who becomes solitary all distances, all measures change; of these changes many take place suddenly, and then, as with the man on the mountaintop, extraordi-

97

nary imaginings and singular sensations arise that seem to grow out beyond all bearing. But it is necessary for us to experience *that* too. We must assume our existence as *broadly* as we in any way can; everything, even the un-heard-of, must be possible in it. That is at bottom the only courage that is demanded of us: to have courage for the most strange, the most singular, and the most inexplicable that we may encounter. That mankind has in this sense been cowardly has done life endless harm; the experiences that are called "visions," the whole so-called "spirit-world," death, all those things that are so closely akin to us, have by daily parrying been so crowded out of life that the senses with which we could have grasped them are atrophied. To say nothing of God.

But fear of the inexplicable has not alone impoverished the existence of the individual; the relationship between one human being and another has also been cramped by it, as though it had been lifted out of the riverbed of endless possibilities and set down in a fallow spot on the bank, to which nothing happens. For it is not inertia alone that is re-sponsible for human relationships repeating themselves from case to case, indescribably monotonous and unre-newed; it is shyness before any sort of new, unforeseeable experience with which one does not think oneself able to cope. But only someone who is ready for everything, who excludes nothing, not even the most enigmatical, will live the relation to another as something alive and will himself draw exhaustively from his own existence. For if we think of this existence of the individual as a larger or smaller room, it appears evident that most people learn to know only a corner of their room, a place by the window, a strip of floor on which they walk up and down. Thus they have a certain security. And yet that dangerous insecurity is so much more human which drives the prisoners in Poe's sto-ries to feel out the shapes of their horrible dungeons and not be strangers to the unspeakable terror of their abode.

We, however, are not prisoners. No traps or snares are set about us, and there is nothing which should intimidate or worry us. We are set down in life as in the element to which we best correspond, and over and above this we have through thousands of years of accommodation become so like this life, that when we hold still we are, through a happy mimicry, scarcely to be distinguished from all that surrounds us. We have no reason to mistrust our world, for it is not against us. Has it terrors, they are *our* terrors; has it abysses, those abysses belong to us; are dangers at hand, we must try to love them. And if only we arrange our life according to that principle which counsels us that we must always hold to the difficult, then that which now still seems to us the most alien will become what we most trust and find most faithful. How should we be able to forget those ancient myths that are at the beginning of all peoples, the myths about dragons that at the last moment turn into princesses; perhaps all the dragons of our lives are princesses who are only waiting to see us once beautiful and brave. Perhaps everything terrible is in its deepest being something helpless that wants help from us.

VII. *The Difficulty of Dying:*
Rilke's Self-Composed Epitaph

Rilke wrote his own epitaph sometime before October 27, 1925 (i.e., about fifteen months before his death), and requested that it be inscribed on his gravestone. This was done and the original headstone, now being restored, will again soon be placed above his grave, on the wall of the church just outside and above the small town of Raron (orignially Rarogne), in the Rhône River valley near Sierre in the canton of Valais in southwest Switzerland.* The epitaph on this stone is given here, along with my translation:

> Rose, oh reiner Widerspruch, Lust,
> Niemandes Schlaf zu sein unter soviel
> Lidern.

> Rose, oh pure contradiction, desire,
> To be no one's sleep under so many
> Lids.

In addition to the usual problems of translation, a special difficulty with my English version of this poem is that *"Lidern"* in German suggests a pun with *"Liedern,"* "songs," a point that will become significant later in my discussion.

---

* This gravestone is not to be confused with another, placed later on the ground of the grave itself by Rilke's daughter, which has a large, simple cross on it. This later stone has become the focus of some controversy. Rilke's aversion to traditional Christianity is well known (the best formal prose statement of his most mature explicit religious views is his brilliant and beautiful essay, "The Young Workman's Letter," written during the great giving, February, 1922). Thus, the cross on the newer gravestone is rather inappropriate, a point of view taken by Rilke's grandson, as related to me by the present occupant of Muzot, who went on to explain that the grandson had told her he wanted it removed. She made it charmingly clear that she agreed with Rilke's grandson, as, I might add, do I.

The poem is about death, as befits an epitaph. And yet death is not mentioned. Rather, the poem speaks throughout of a rose, that great old poetic symbol. But the rose addressed by the first word of the poem is not Dante's rose, or even one of the great rose windows of medieval cathedrals, about which Rilke himself wrote a lovely poem. Still less is it Robert Burns' rose, or William Blake's, or Gertrude Stein's, or Robert Frost's. But perhaps Rilke's rose is not that distant—the rose a lover gives his beloved is also the rose of death, for, as Rilke says, lovers, *"being full of life, . . . are full of death";* and elsewhere, "So *deep* is death implanted in the nature of love that . . . it nowhere contradicts love." The traditional lover's rose, however, rarely makes this connection evident, which is one distinction between it and Rilke's rose.

For, from the beginning, Rilke's rose was a deeper figure, a more primal reality, moving toward the unity of life and death. In a poem written at the age of twenty (and included in *Advent* [1898]), Rilke makes some traditional correspondences, even some rather sentimentally romantic ones, between roses and love: e.g., "I am braiding tired roses / in your hair" ["ich dir müde Rosen flechte / ins Haar"]. But even here there is a difference. *"Tired* roses" would suggest a *fin de siècle* sensibility were it not for the later direction of the poem, where the roses almost become a crown of "dark thorns" ["dunkle Dornen"] and the poet asks, "Do you feel the roses dying on your brow?" ["Fühlst du die Rosen auf der Stirne sterben?"]. Even to this point, there is little to distinguish the sentiment. But the poem closes with the declaration, "And we are roses'-heirs" ["Und wir sind Rosenerben"], and with that a new dimension is opened up. The links between love and death and love and rose are fairly traditional, but this final line points to a deeper insight—though it points only. A quarter century of exploration down that more difficult path would follow, some few signposts of which can be seen in a number of the poems on roses, other flowers, blossoming, and growth included in this volume (see, e.g., pp. 45, 51, 67, 71, 79).

The rose invoked in Rilke's epitaph was discovered only far down that path, however. This begins to become apparent in the next phrase of the poem: "oh pure contradiction." Again, if one makes the traditional association, one would think the poet is speaking of that standard contradiction between the beauty of the rose and the thorns which protect that beauty. But no, the contradiction is a pure one, that is, it resides in the bloom itself, not between the blossom and the stem. The contradiction is within the very heart of the blossoming rose itself. It is of the essence of the rose. *What?*

The next word begins to speak of the nature of that contradiction. And yet that word is a strange and unexpected one, and is unusually punctuated: "desire," concluding the line with a stop by means of a comma. This word, with its placement, with its being set off by commas, not only suggests an identity; that is, rose = pure contradiction = desire. But much more is also being suggested here: rose, which can be more carefully understood as pure contradiction, which can be further perceived as desire. And still further, the position of the word "desire" points not only back to the pure contradiction and the rose but forward to the next line as well. But not unambiguously forward; one might even say not uncontradictorily forward—for there is the comma, the last punctuation until the final period. This suggests that the rest of the poem still further descriptively specifies the nature of desire-contradiction-rose.

The word "desire" itself does some work on its own. It suggests one of the major concerns of this volume: love. Now we can see why the traditional associations between love and rose are only tangentially related to this rose. For desire, as a form of or pointer to love, is not usually thought of as involving a contradiction. And yet this desire is so linked. But again, the nature of the contradiction remains unclear. Still less is it clear at this point what desire has to do with an epitaph, with death.

So one moves to the final lines of the poem. "To be" emphasizes what was already hinted at, that the essence of the rose is being spoken. It is the being, not merely the appearance, of the rose, and indeed of pure contradiction and of desire, that is being presented here. It is the depth, not merely the surface. Or, rather, as we shall see, it is the being of the rose *as it appears;* it is the depth visible on the surface. And at that depth one discovers "no one's sleep." At last one hears a word one might expect in an epitaph. Sleep is an ordinary, even sentimentally trite euphemism for death. But this sleep has nothing in common with such sentiment. It is not a dead, faded rose. The rose is in full bloom and the sleep is the dying sleep which is the living rose itself.

As always, trite and traditional associations get in one's way. It is easy to say that death comes to all at the end. It is a bit more difficult to hear that one begins to die the minute one is born. Still more difficult is to see that life always goes toward death and that dying is an intimate and lively part of living. Most difficult of all is the effort of *"affirmation of life-and-death as one,"* to quote Rilke. "Our effort," he said, "can *only* go toward postulating the unity of life and death, so that it may gradually prove itself to us." This is that most difficult task Rilke has characteristically taken upon himself. Death is not an event tacked onto one's life, constituting the end of that life. It is rather the ever-present "other side of life," as Rilke so often declared. In his epitaph, he is attempting to portray—indeed, to make present —the reality of this frequent declaration. Thus, the sleep belongs most intimately to the blossoming rose. This is part of the contradiction.

Another is that it is *"no one's* sleep." Death is the other side of *life,* not just of *my* life. In death, as in life, one participates in—indeed, *touches*—domains far beyond that of the personal, the individual. Which is not to suggest the impersonal, or even the transpersonal as such. The sleep is no one's, yet it belongs intimately to the rose. The domain is simultaneously life and the other side of life. And this is not merely a fact. One must grow toward . . . . . this desire, to be, no one's, sleep. So there *is* a special link between desire and sleep, love and death. But it constitutes a difficulty. It requires an effort. It is something one must grow toward and achieve. The achievement occurs, however, only *in* the growing, the living. In fact, desiring to be no one's sleep *is* growing, *is* living. This is the affirmation of life-*and*-death. But that "no one" still puzzles. Perhaps the final words will help.

But they present still another contradiction. This difficult effort to achieve—indeed, to become—the desire to be no one's sleep is at the same time the most natural and most intimate thing of all. For it is a sleep "under so many / Lids." These concluding words appear enigmatic until one remembers the focus of the poem. The rose is a mystery. Soft velvet petals, each curling over and gesturing other petals, which in turn protect still others, which finally curve around . . . . . nothing. Rilke had long been fascinated by that circling nothing, that mysterious silence—so full and so resonant—at the heart of a rose. In his poem "The Rose Window" ["Die Fensterrose"], from *New Poems,* to which I referred above, his gaze is transfixed by the returning stare of the window: "the glance which, as though caught by a whirlpool's / circling, swims a little while" ["den Blick, der, wie von eines Wirbels Kreis / ergriffen, eine kleine Weile schwimmt"]. In another, most important rose poem from the same volume, "The Bowl of Roses" ["Die Rosenschale"], this curling-into-nothing essence of the rose is made explicit:

And this: that one opens like a lid,
and lying under there nothing but eyelids,
closed, as if they, tenfold sleeping,
had to muffle an inner power of seeing.

[Und dies: daß eins sich aufschlägt wie ein Lid,
und drunter liegen lauter Augenlider,
geschlossene, als ob sie, zehnfach schlafend,
zu dämpfen hätten eines Innern Sehkraft.]

Here too, as in the epitaph, the petals of a rose are shown
to be eyelids, covering a resonant silence, an alert sleep.
But this is of the very nature of a rose—indeed, of the sheer
appearance of the rose. (*Sic transit* Kant.) The petals actu-
ally do curve over into each other. And there really is nothing under all those petals, a nothing which is destroyed
when the botanist examines the rose. Thus, the very "objec-
tive" nature of a rose is the concrete, and at the same time
mysterious, figure of precisely what Rilke wants his gravestone to speak. Or, rather, Rilke has so pondered the rose,
has so let it be, that it has revealed its very essence to him.
This contradictory little flower:—awake and yet asleep, seeing and yet with eyelids closed, living and dying.

Yet that . . . . . space, there is no other word—that space
within the rose is not empty. That nothing is not merely no
thing. It sees. It speaks. It has—or rather, is—an inner eye-
sight, an inner power or force or strength of seeing. It reso-
nates and vibrates, like those other Rilkean figures—the
space where the water of a fountain has ceased to rise but
has not yet begun to fall, and the same space of the flight
of a child's ball thrown into the air. So with the sleep of a
rose: it is not some-thing, some object, but it is not an
empty nothing either. Rilke had a beautiful word for this—
"*Weltinnenraum,*" "world-inner-space." It is most often used
to speak that essential space within the heart of a human
being. But the very word itself, *world*-inner-space, suggests

a link between that space and the sleep at the heart of the rose, the shimmering space above the jet of a fountain. In a letter, Rilke speaks of this as the "space untouched as the inside of a rose, an angelic space in which one keeps still." And in *Sonnets to Orpheus* (II, 6), he even calls this space in the rose a "body of nothing but radiance" ["Leib aus nichts als Glanz"].

The sleep is no one's. It is the plenitude of the nothing of both the world-sleep in the center of the rose and the vibrant innerness that dwells in the being of man. Still another poem from *New Poems* has the very title "Rose-Innerness" ["Das Rosen-Innere"], and begins by asking, "Where for this inner is / an outer?" ["Wo ist zu diesem Innen / ein Außen?"]. The epitaph does more than answer this question. It presents the union of inner and outer, sleeping and waking, nothing and being (that ancient philosophical contradiction), yes, and of life and death. And the union of what is already joined is accomplished through the motive power of desire, the power which is desire. Yet a contradiction remains, for the inner and outer are not identical—the space is gone the minute one peels away the petals. The sleep is invisible. It is no one's. Nonetheless, around it is the rose fashioned. And the desire which *is* the pure contradiction and the rose is not a desire *for* something merely, but is a desiring being. The desire which is the life of the rose is the contradiction of gesturing, of being, this sleep.

So this is Rilke's rose. And, as he said in the first of the *Duino Elegies,* "Indeed it is strange . . . / not to give roses, and other properly promising things / the significance of a human future" ["Freilich ist es seltsam . . . / Rosen, und andern eigens versprechenden Dingen / nicht die Bedeutung menschlicher Zukunft zu geben"]. Strange indeed. Rilke's rose does have the significance of a human future. Because he took upon himself the task of seeing the rose. And yet, at the same time, dying is *now*, says the rose.

All of this is presented, is made present, in Rilke's epitaph. It is not spoken about. It is not even portrayed or described. It is set before us. And it is placed on Rilke's grave. So we come to the final dimension of the poem. It is the epitaph of a poet—indeed, of one whose last long sequence of poems was to the singing god, Orpheus. And this too is hinted at in the last word of the epitaph, so strangely placed as though for emphasis and reflection: *"Lidern"* = "lids," suggesting, as I mentioned earlier, *"Liedern"* = "songs." Thus the epitaph is *Rilke's,* the man, the poet. Above all, it is the epitaph for the poet's work, his poems, his singing. But the poet is not Orpheus. He is rather the messenger who speaks the words of Orpheus. For Orpheus himself is the rose. As Rilke sang in *Sonnets to Orpheus* (I, 5):

> Erect no memorial stone. Just let the rose
> bloom each year on his behalf.
> For it is Orpheus.

> [Errichtet keinen Denkstein. Laßt die Rose
> nur jedes Jahr zu seinen Gunsten blühn.
> Denn Orpheus ists.]

Orpheus—the singing god who goes to the realm of the dead for love—is the rose. Or the rose is the series of petals, lids, songs, which, from desire, is no one's sleep—which is Orpheus. And the final contradiction is that once the journey is made, once the rose is dead, all that remains are the songs, the words, "an earned word, pure" ["ein erworbenes Wort, reines" (*Duino Elegies,* IX)]. All that remains is the poem, the figure. "But let us rejoice a while now / to believe the figure. That's enough." ["Doch uns freue eine Weile nun, / der Figur zu glauben. Das genügt." (*Sonnets to Orpheus,* I, 11)].

"Then," said Malte, "quite at the end, one might perhaps be able to write ten lines that were good." In his own epitaph, in scarcely more than ten words, Rilke wrote his one poem, the one poem that each poet seeks, a poem which achieves the "one task set clearly" before Rilke, as he himself expressed it: "To confirm confidence toward death out of the deepest delights and glories of life: to make death, who never was a stranger, more distinct and palpable again as the silent knowing participant in everything alive."

VIII. *Epilogue*

IT HAS BEEN FIFTY YEARS since Rilke's great giving. I am tempted to call this volume of offering a work of commemoration. But Rilke is too alive for memorials. Or one could say we need Rilke too much to solemnize him. We have too far to go in the directions he pointed toward and explored for us to place him on the shelf of reverence.

Take, for example, just two lines from his last two extensive works. From the fourth of the *Duino Elegies*: "Murderers are / easily comprehended" ["Mörder sind / leicht einzusehen"]. And from *Sonnets to Orpheus* (II, 11): *"Killing is a form of our wandering mourning . . ."* [*"Töten ist eine Gestalt unseres wandernden Trauerns . . ."*]. This seems so incomprehensible to us, so strange, so counter to all our usual moral judgments and expectations. One translator even flippantly and insultingly reduces the line from the *Sonnets* to a level which even Voltaire would not bother to satirize ("Whatever is, is right"). In this century of madness and murder, one would have thought that readers of Rilke, and, still more, his translators, would perceive the reality he is speaking in these lines, if nothing else. Perhaps others' words can help. Norman O. Brown says it this way:

A social order which draws a distinction between the wish and the deed, between the criminal and the righteous, is still a kingdom of darkness. It is only as long as a distinction is made between real and imaginary murders that real murders are worth committing. (*Love's Body*, p. 152)

Samuel Beckett says it this way:

and that linked thus bodily together each one of us is at the same time Bom and Pim tormentor and tormented pedant and dunce wooer and wooed speechless and reafflicted with speech in the dark in the mud nothing to emend there (*How It Is*, p. 140)

And Jesus said it this way:

"You have heard that it was said to the men of old, 'You shall not kill; and whoever kills shall be liable to judgment.' But I say to you that every one who is angry with his brother shall be liable to judgment; whoever insults his brother shall be liable to the council, and whoever says, 'You fool!' shall be liable to the hell of fire." (Matt. 5: 21–22)

Are not we all angry and insulting and do not we all see ourselves as tormented ones only, not the tormentors? And we certainly distinguish between "real" and "imaginary" murders. So we cannot even say with Rilke that we understand murderers. And we surely would not admit that "killing is a form of our wandering mourning." For we do not know the murderer within.

The remarkable thing about this aspect of Rilke's work is that it is so minor, presented almost by the way. What is for us so difficult is for Rilke an insight to be presented only in passing, as he goes on to explore the really difficult mysteries. Yes indeed, how greatly we need the quietly radical Rilke.

In lifting up just this one aspect of Rilke's poetic thinking as I looked over what I have done here, I felt torn. There is so very much more to say. So many other things need to be spoken, so many more central dimensions need to be lifted up and pondered. At one point or another in my discussions here, I have mentioned many of them: major images, basic concerns, fundamental figures. But they need to be *thought into*—not thought through; we are hardly ready for that. And they need to be thought into slowly and care-fully in relation to life.

Even more important is the movement in Rilke's work. As we saw with Rilke's rose, so with all other concerns of his poetry: there is a deepening development, a nurtured growth. Perhaps no poet, not even Yeats, grew poetically as much as Rilke. And we need to think that nurtured growth.

And so with this volume. Here too is a curve, an arc, flung out into the world and followed in into one's self. This line became manifest to me only as I was deep into the work. The line of this book moves from love through all the many complex and complexly interwoven dimensions of the poems of Part IV, to blood-remembering (an explicit suggestion as to how all this might be related to one's own everyday existence), and finally to death, which was of course present at the start and throughout (see, e.g., the sixth phallic poem and the many poems in Part IV in which death is considered). I only point to this line now, as I have only pointed to so many other things here. I am not yet ready to think it. Another book is surely called for.

My work here, then, is only a beginning, as I indicated in the Prologue. Or perhaps it is only the beginning of a beginning. My hope is that the beginning will be a real one—for me, so that I can find more words to take me further toward my deeper sense of Rilke, and for others who will also then be impelled to return to Rilke and ponder his poetry. Perhaps just that much would make this volume valuable both for me and for those who read it. That much would be sufficient—for beginning is perhaps the most difficult thing of all.

And we, who think of *mounting*
happiness, would feel the emotion
which nearly startles
when happiness *falls*.

Explore transformation throughout.
What is your most suffering experience?
Is drinking bitter to you, turn to wine.

.   .   .

And if the earthly forgot you,
to the still earth say: I run.
To the swift water speak: I am.